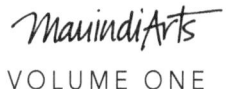

VOLUME ONE

TRANQUILITY
PATTERNS
COLOURING BOOK

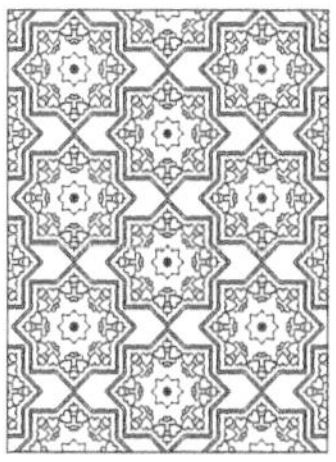

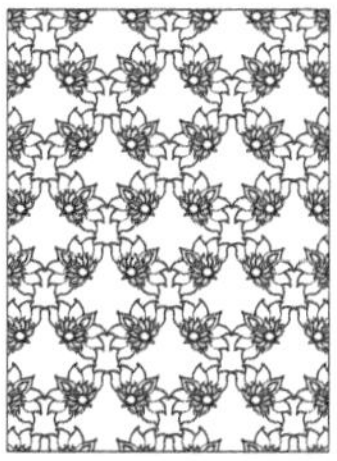

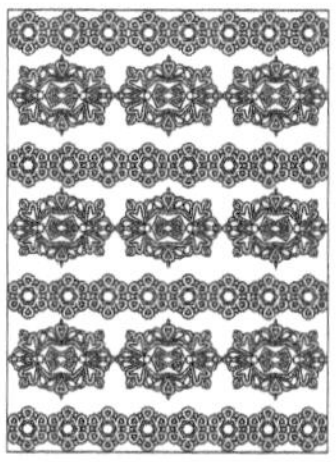

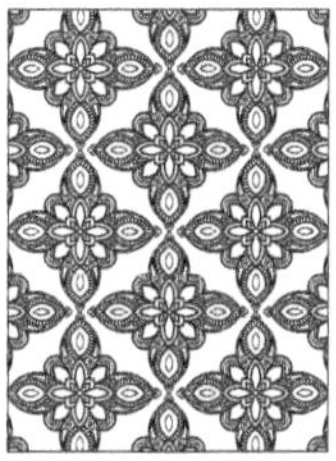

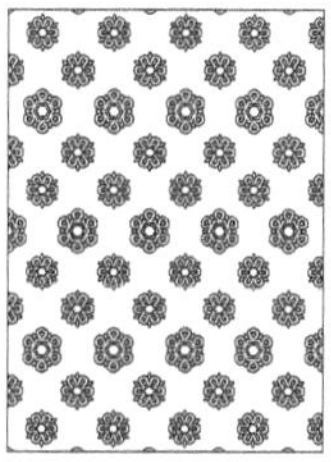

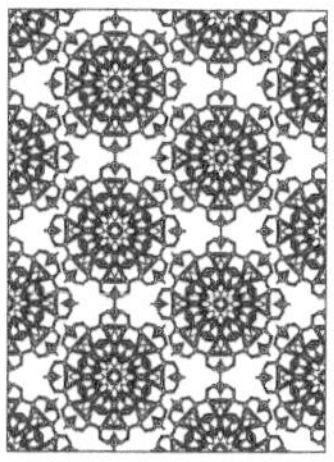

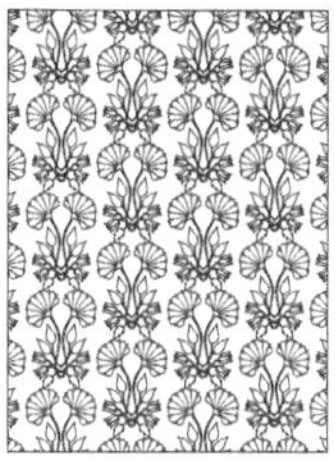

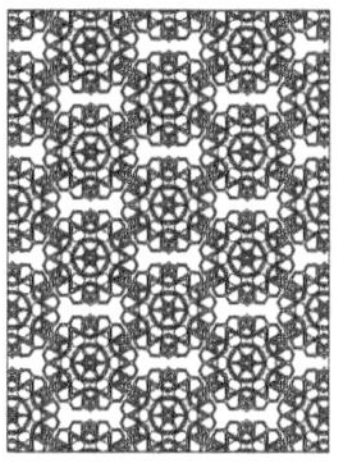

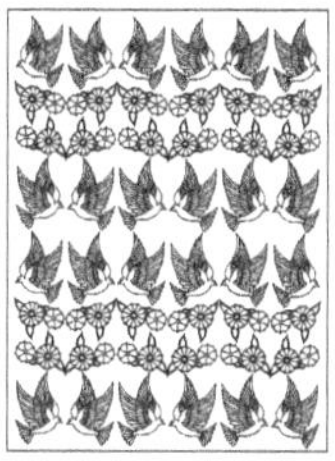

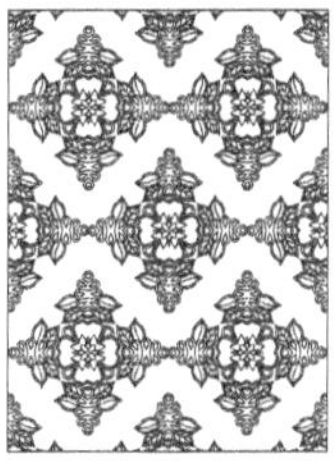

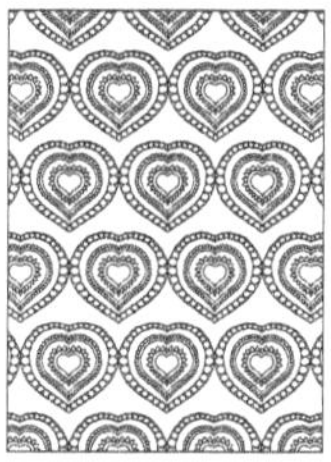

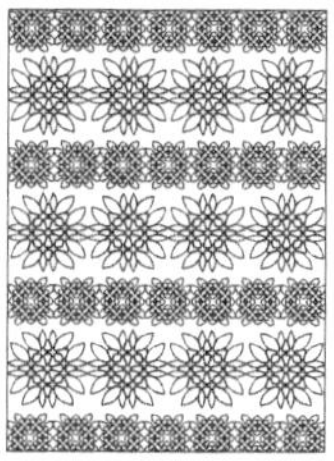

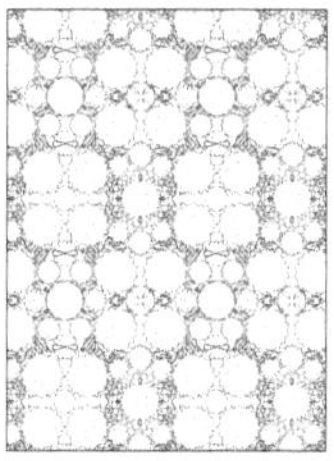

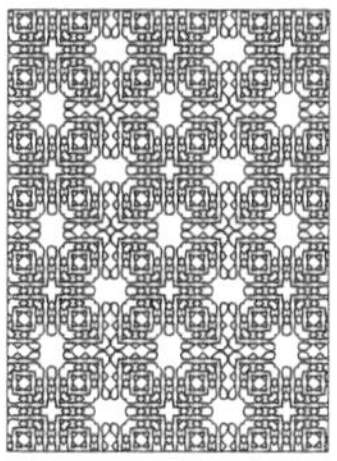

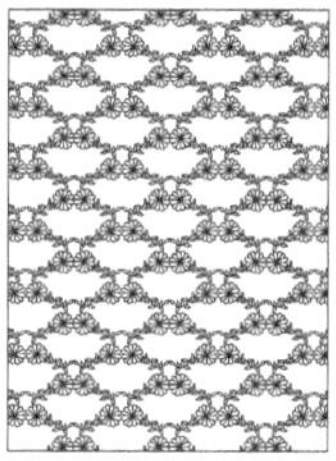

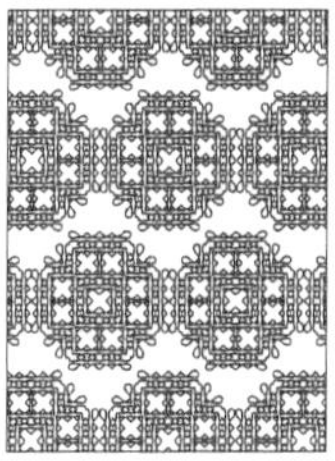

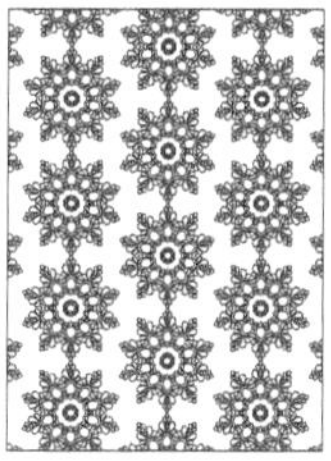

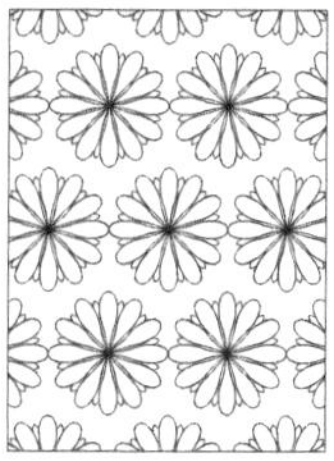

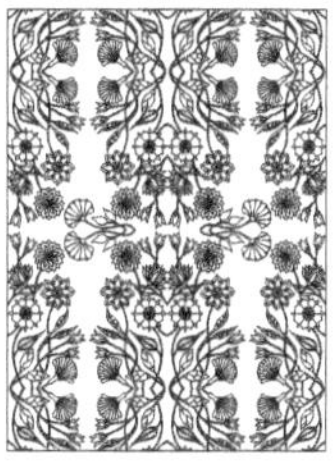

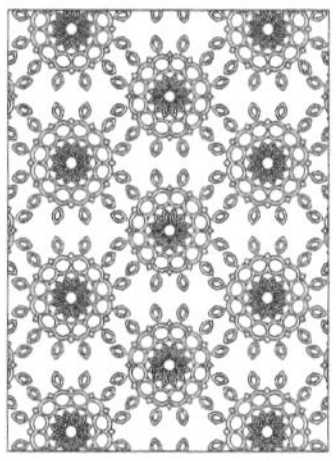

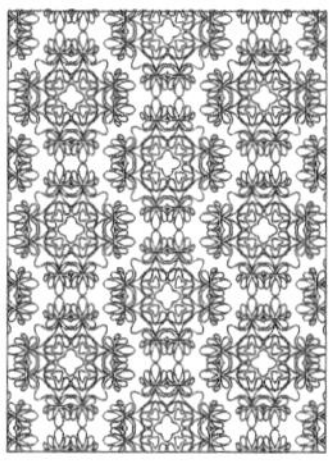

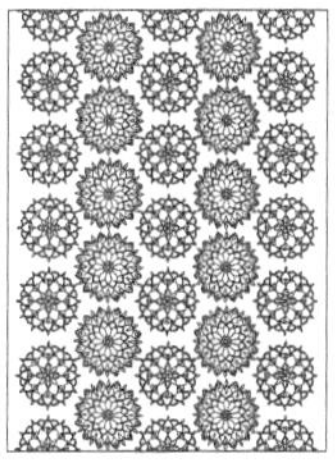

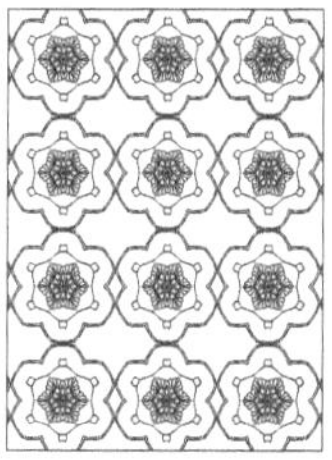

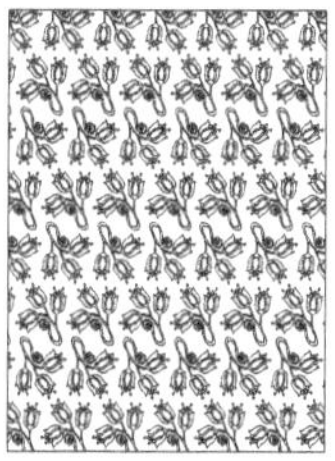

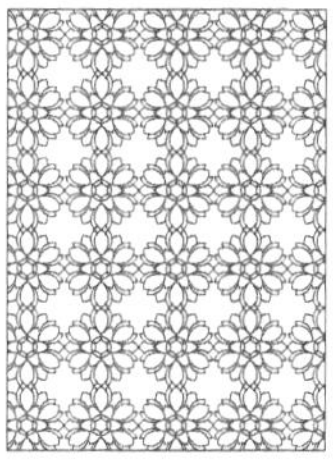

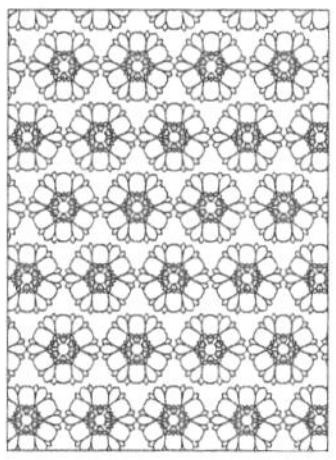

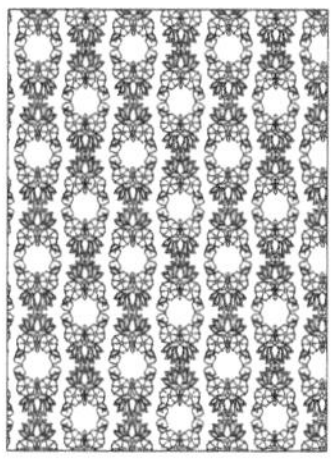

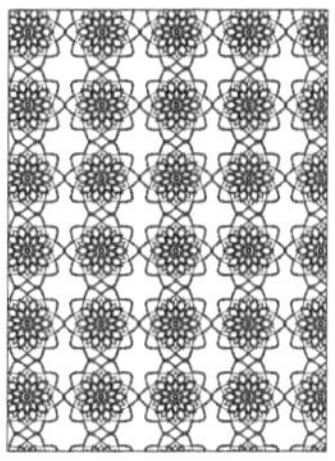

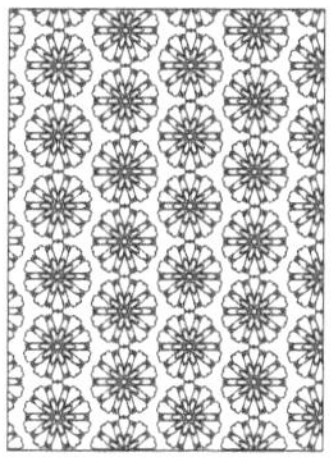

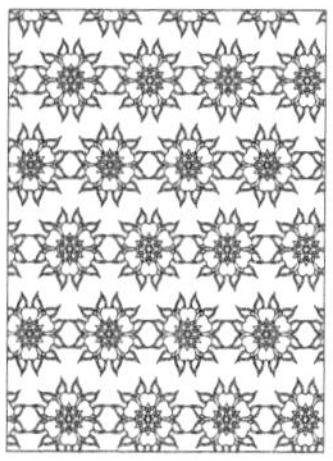

More at **www.etsy.com/au/shop/MauindiArts.** Find us on Facebook: **www.facebook.com/MauindiArts**

www.mauindiarts.com

© MauindiArts 2015

ISBN-13: 978-1532953194

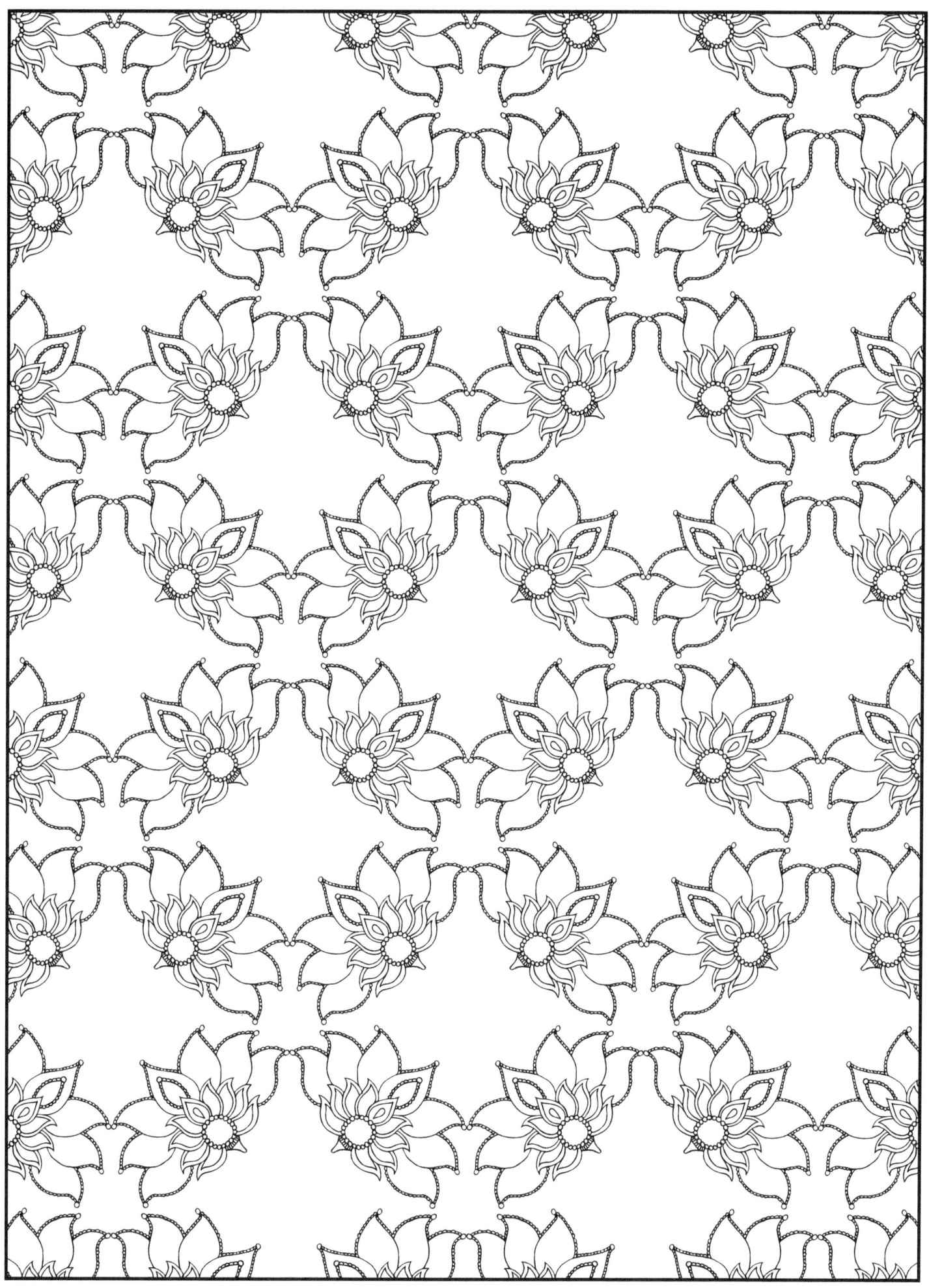

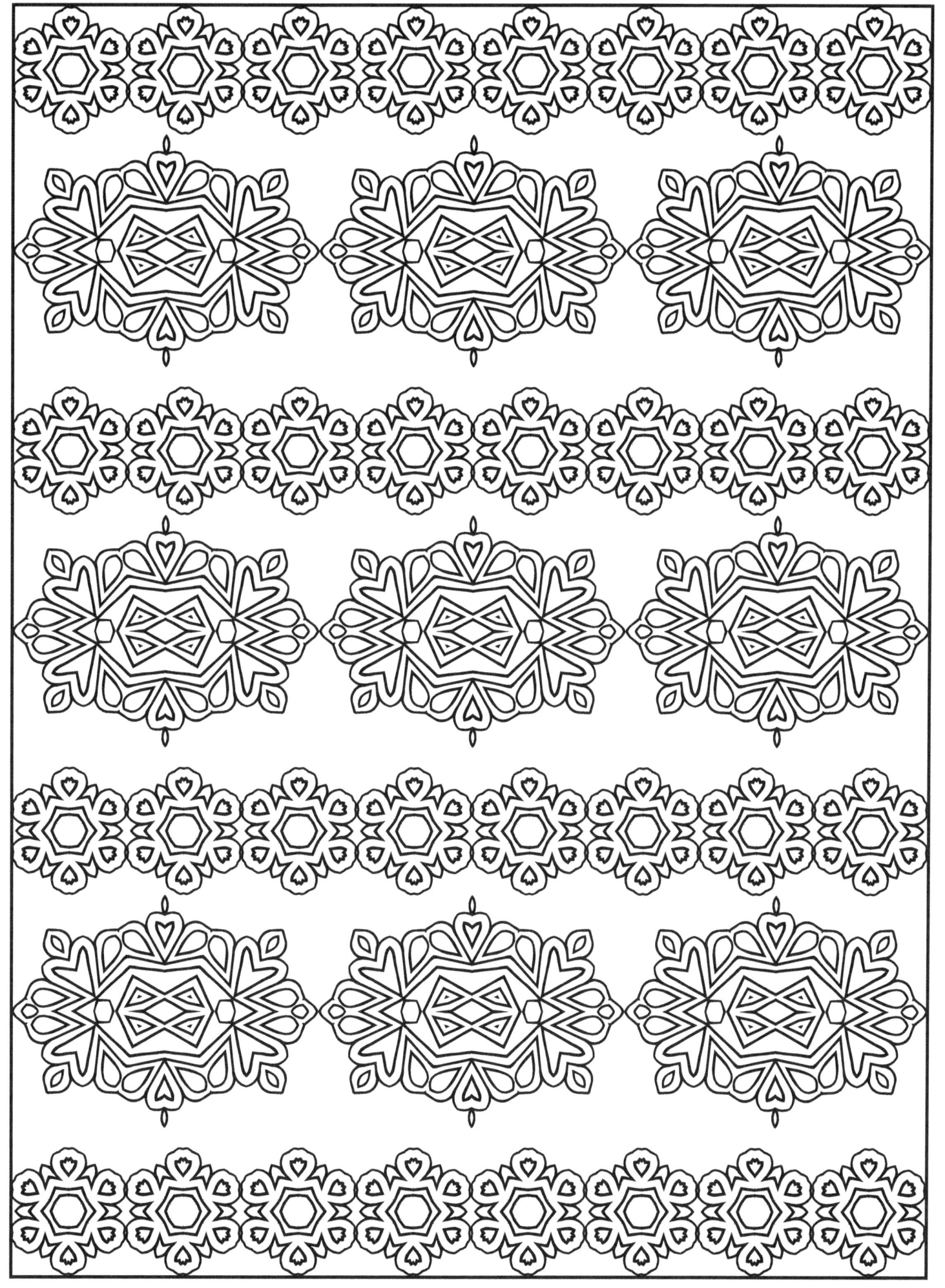

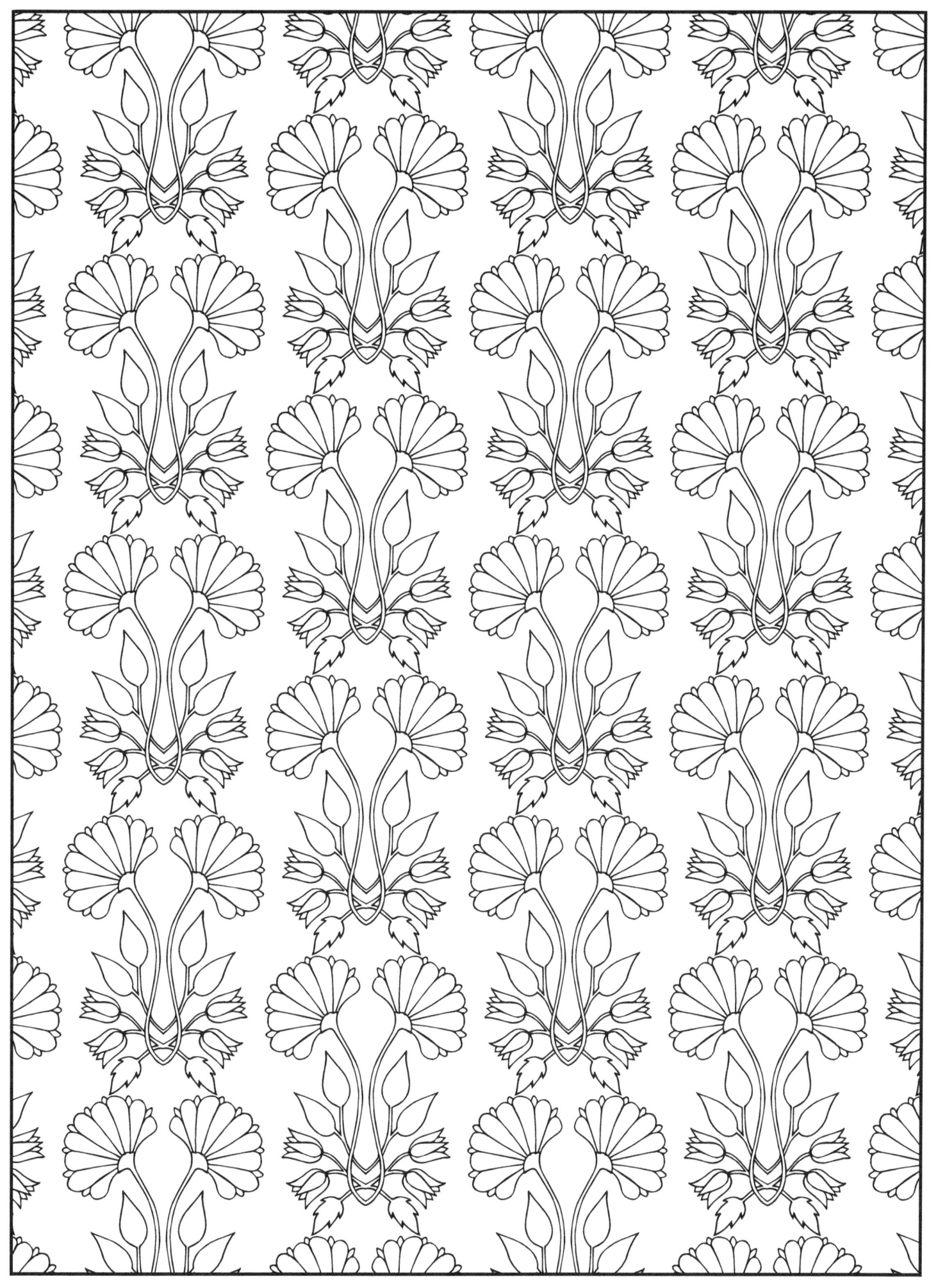

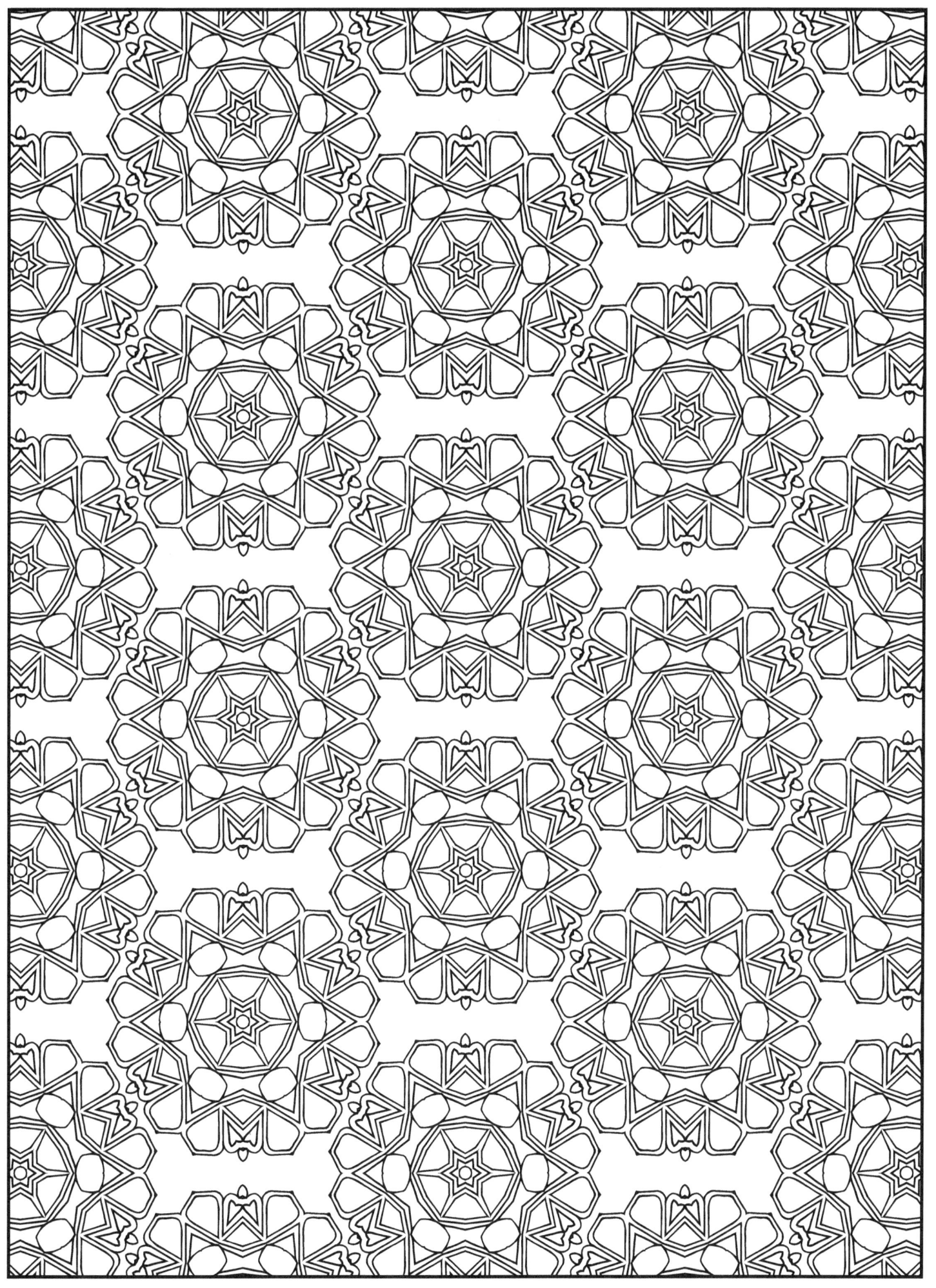

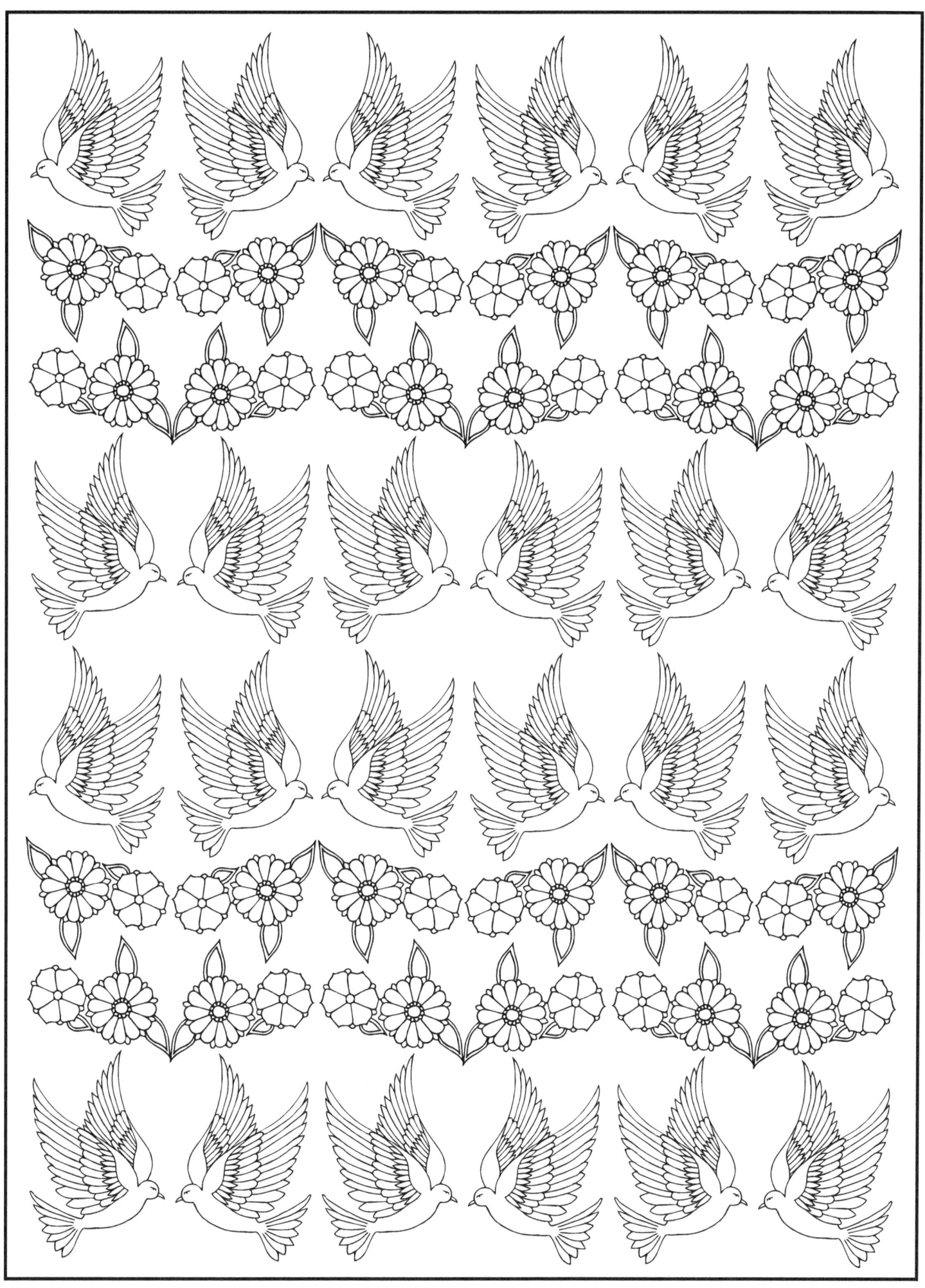

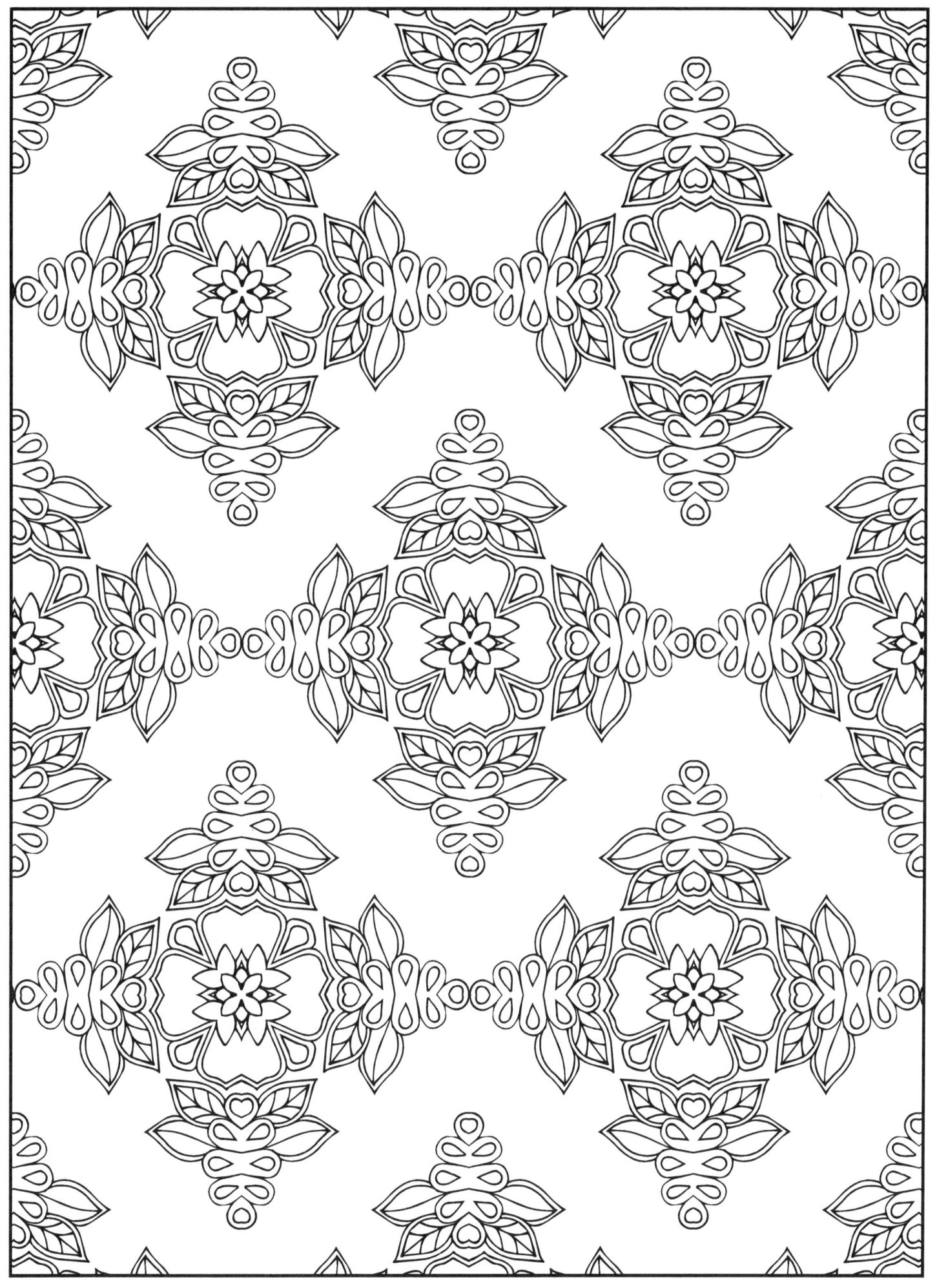

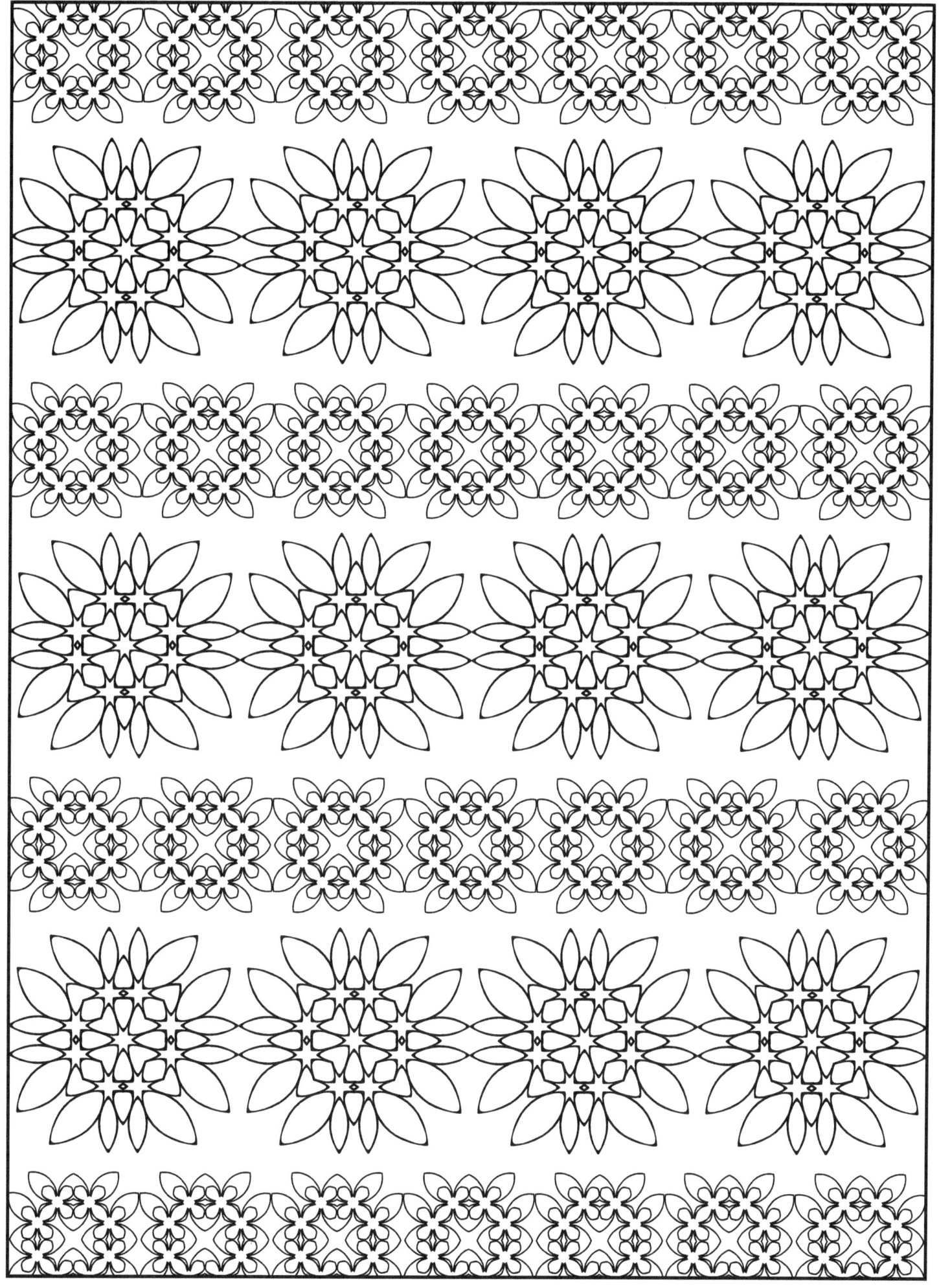

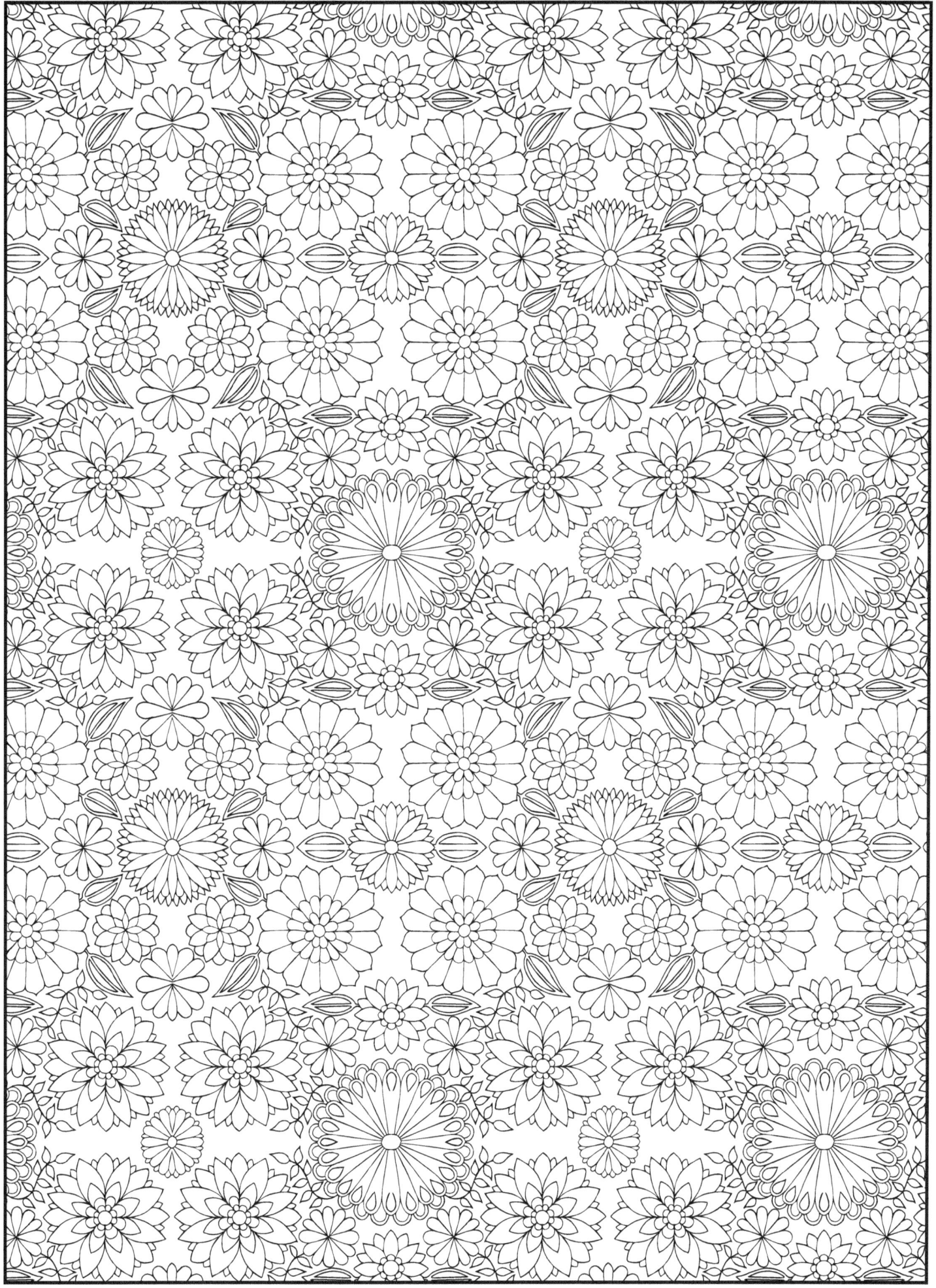

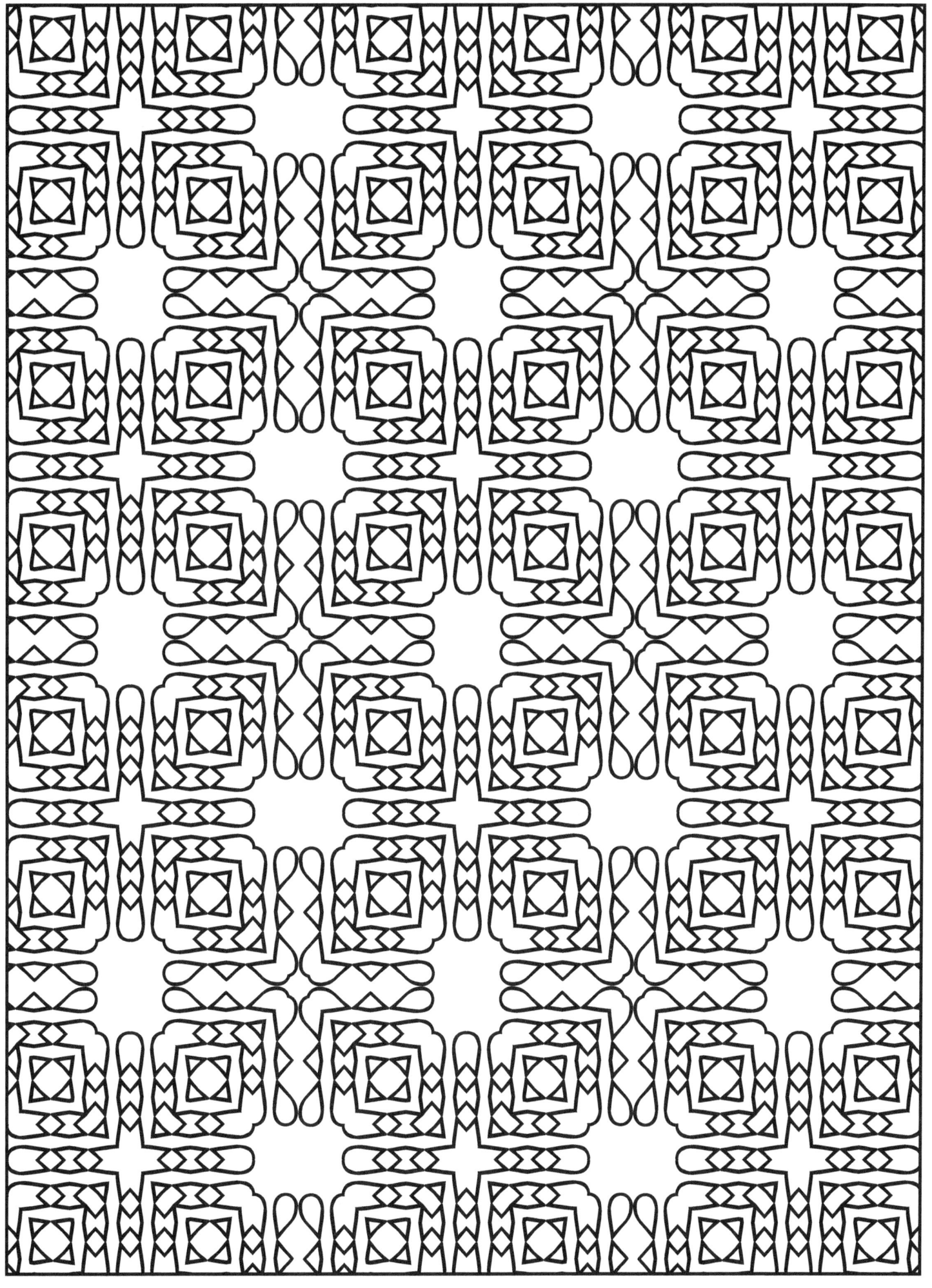

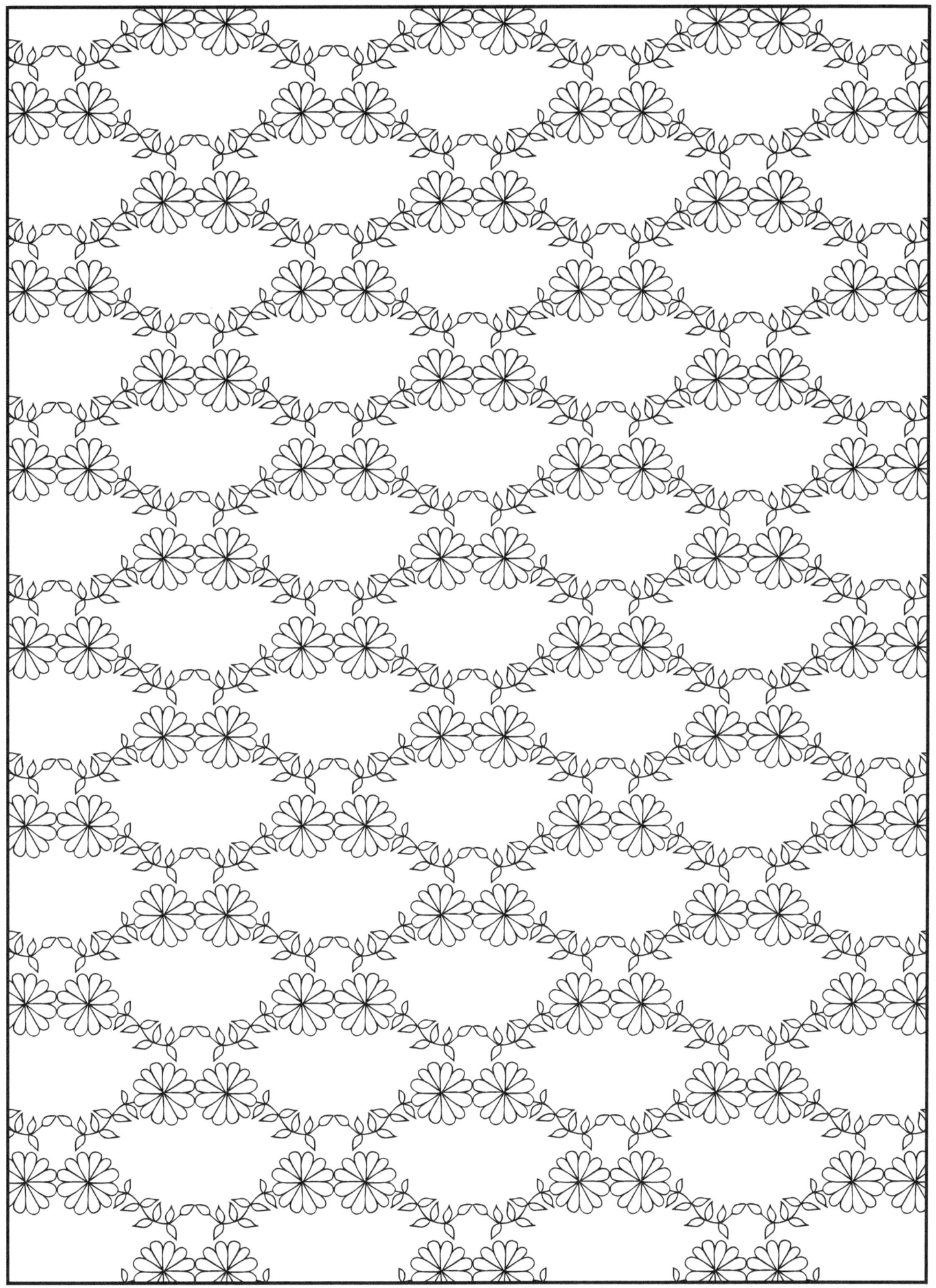

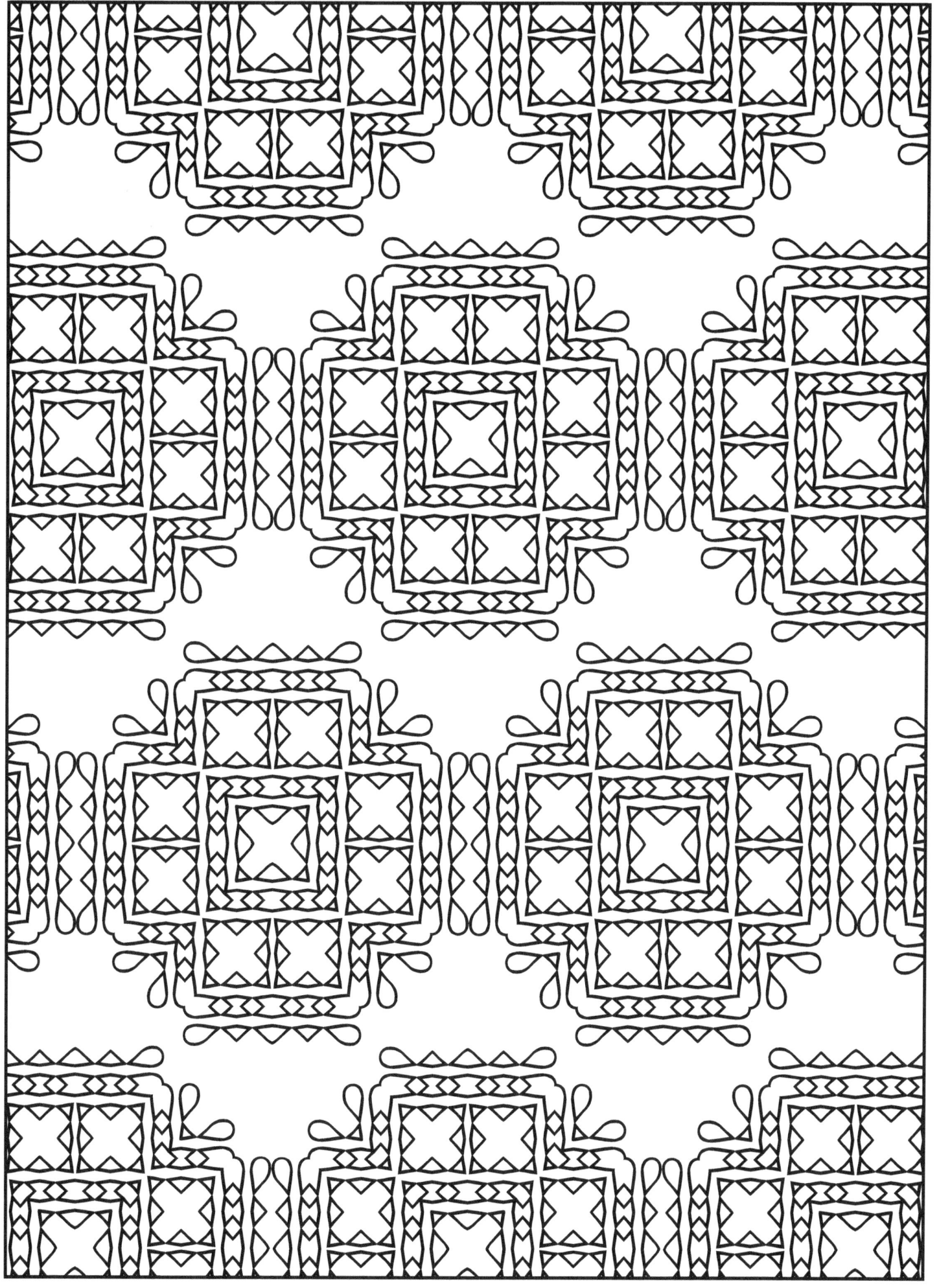

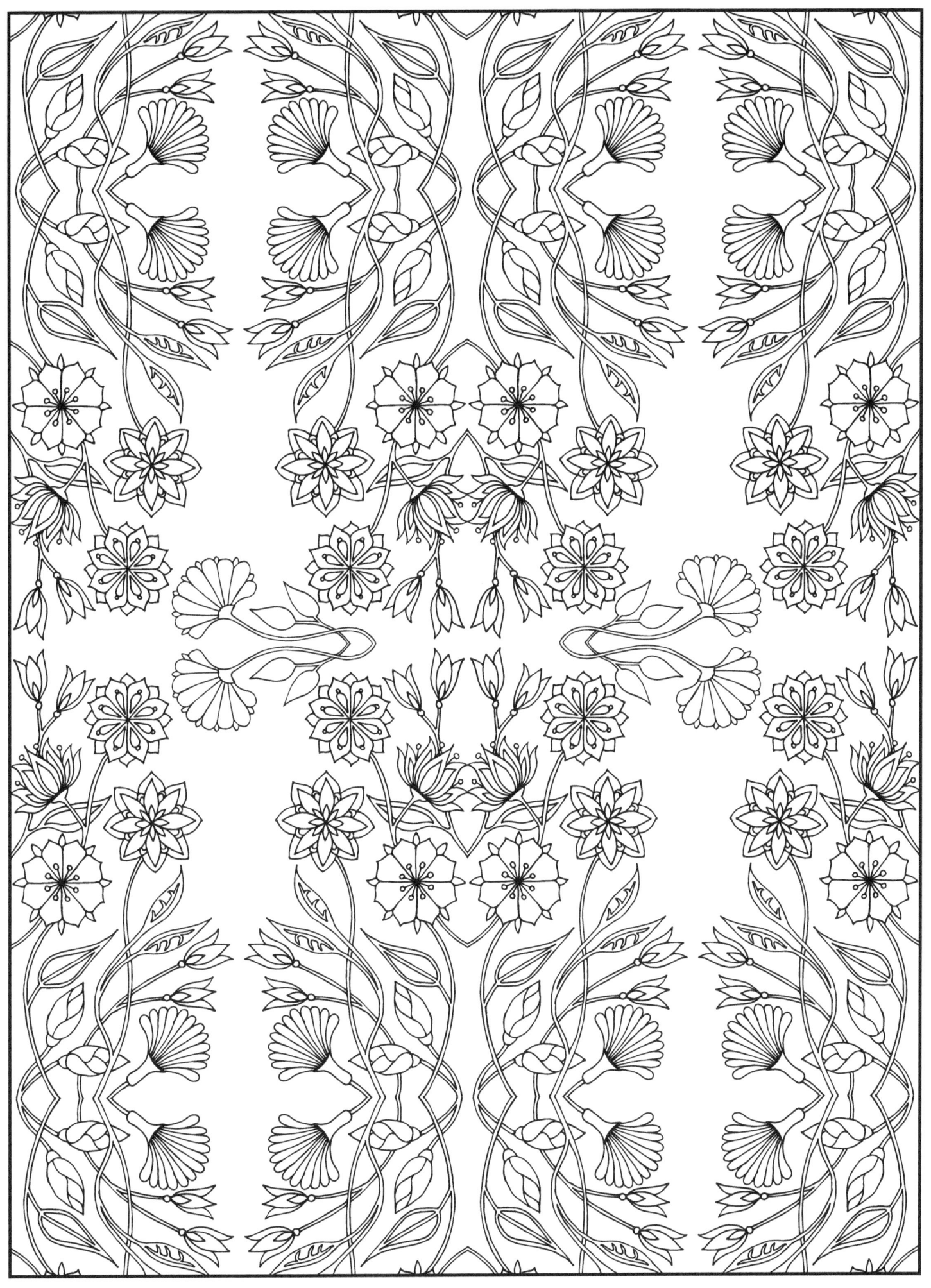

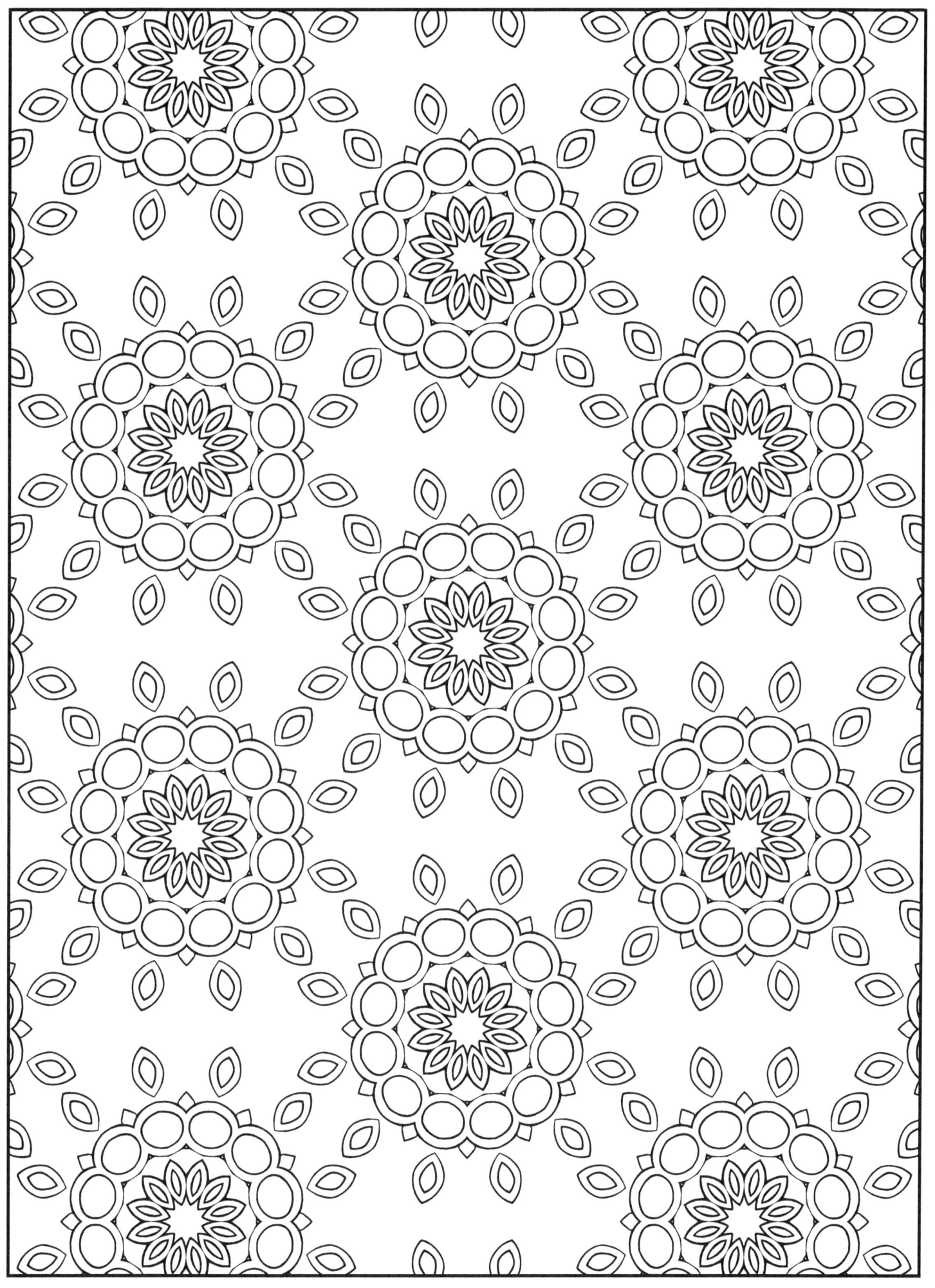

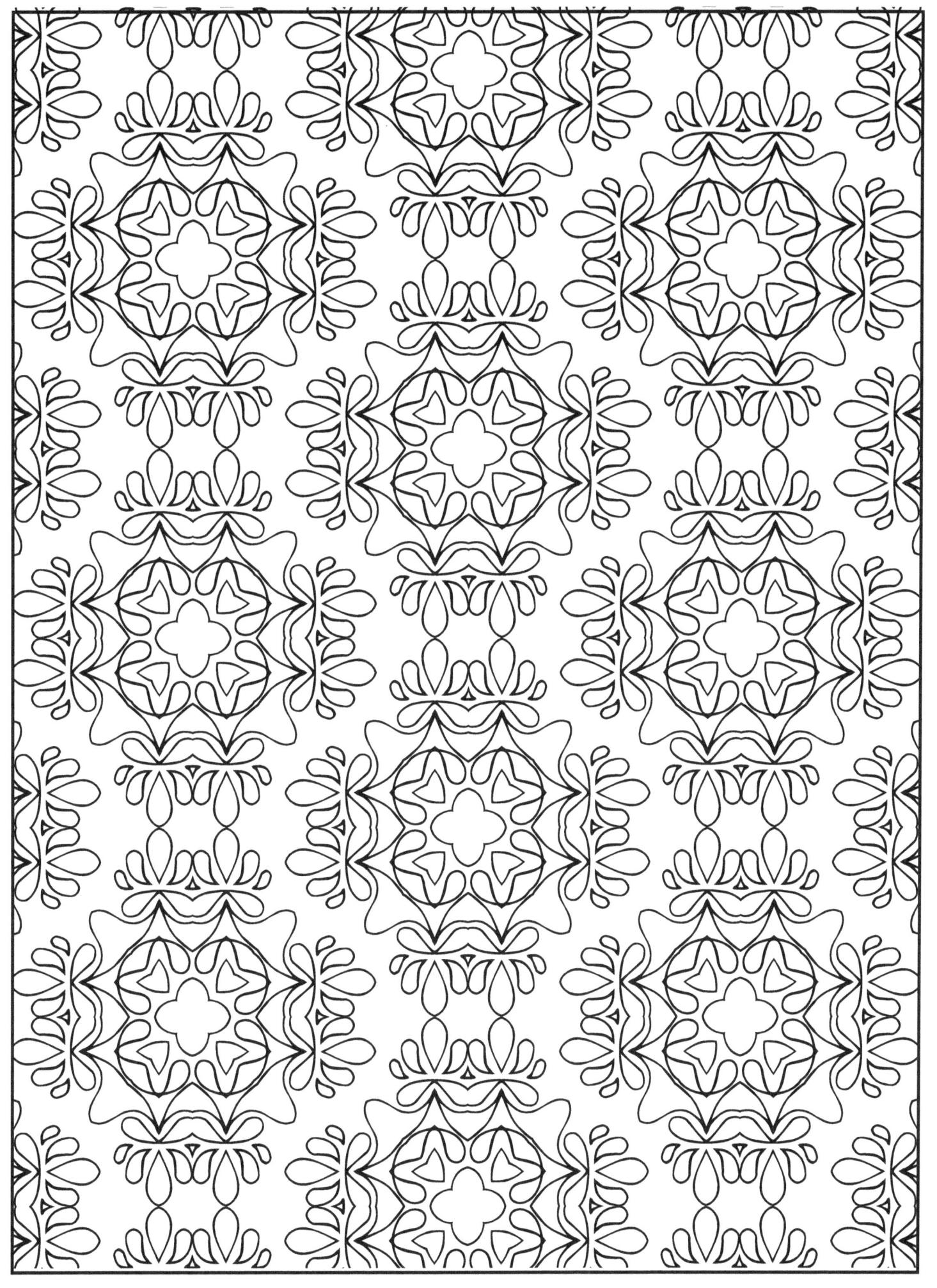

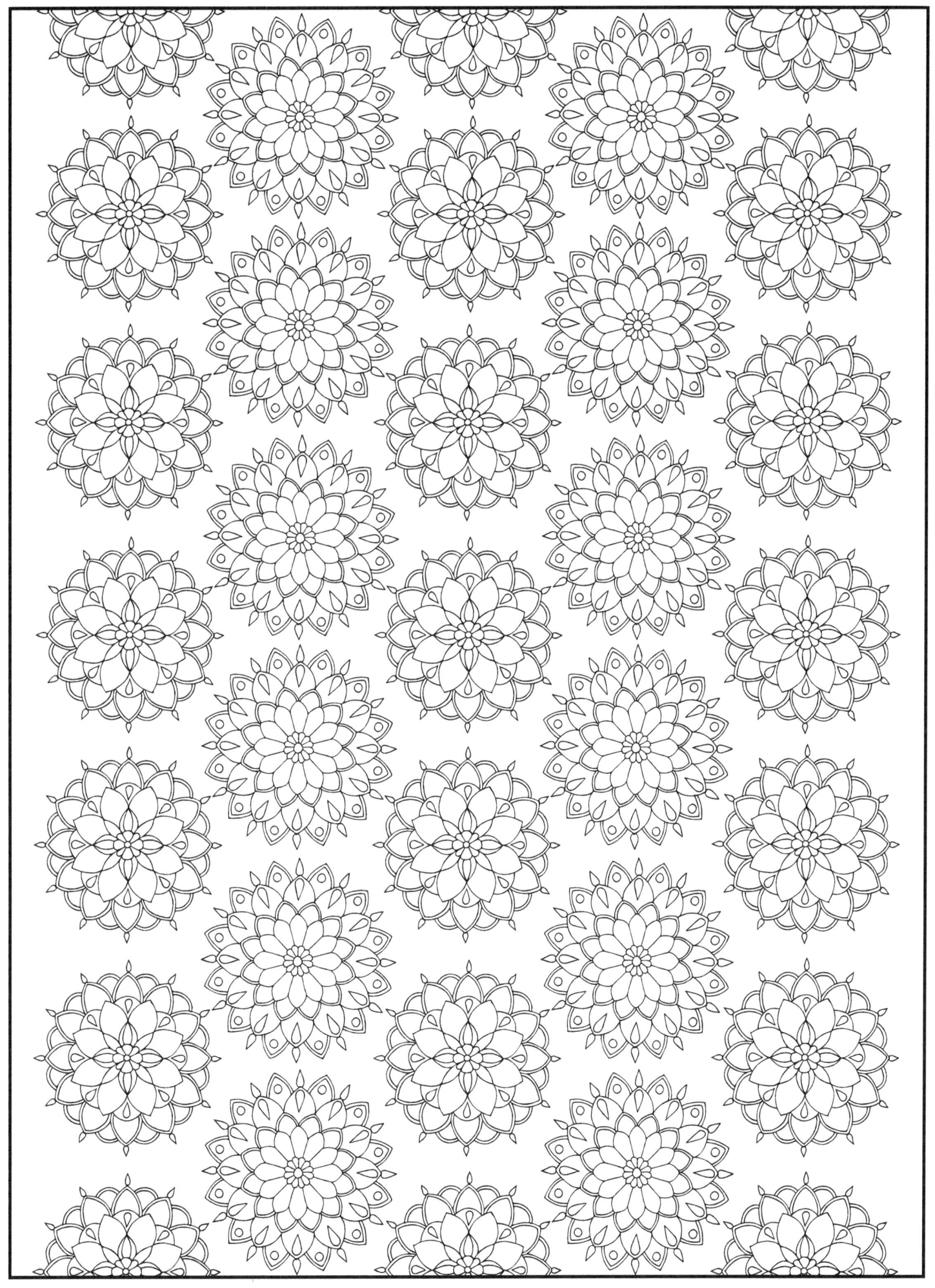

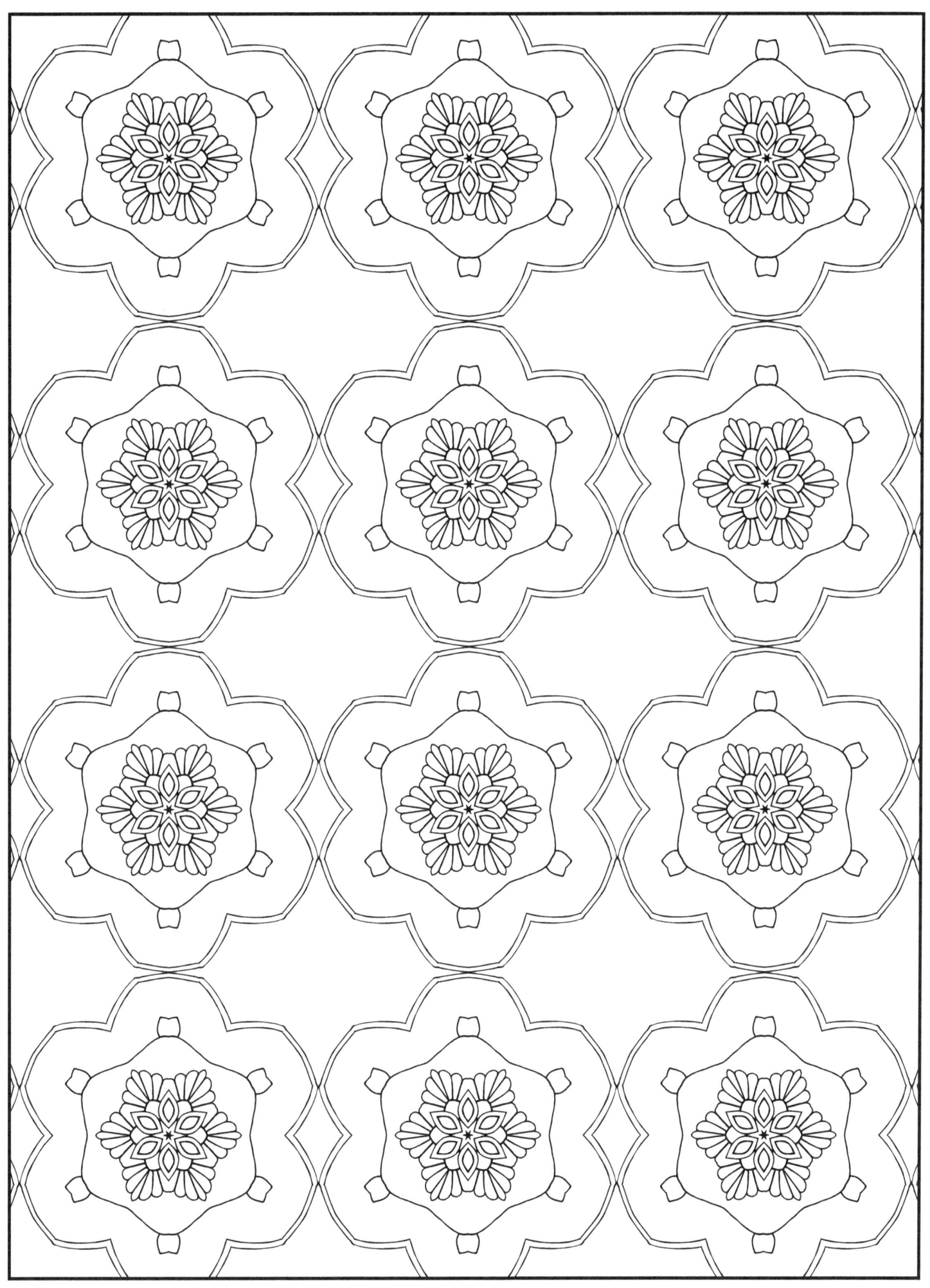

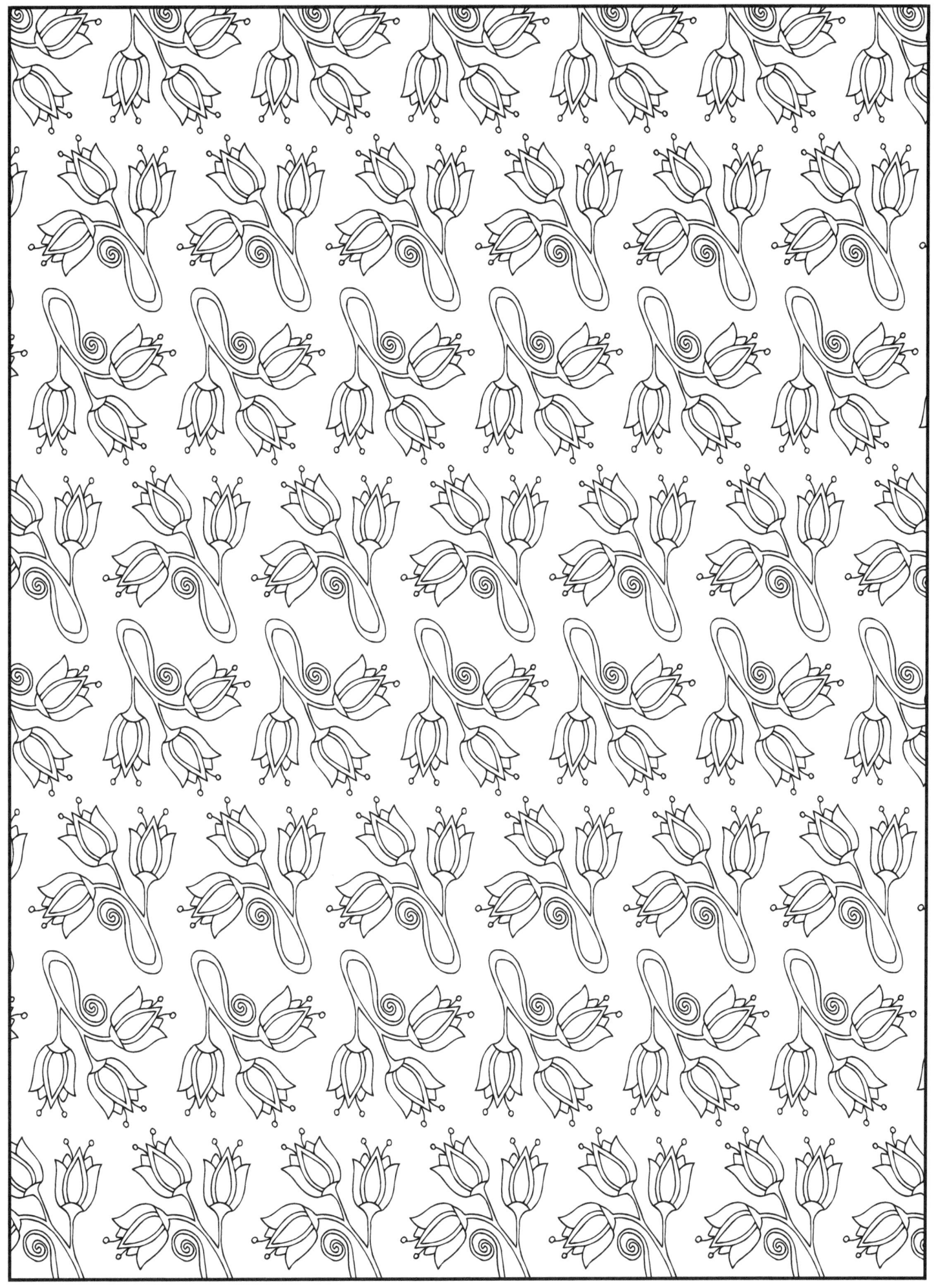

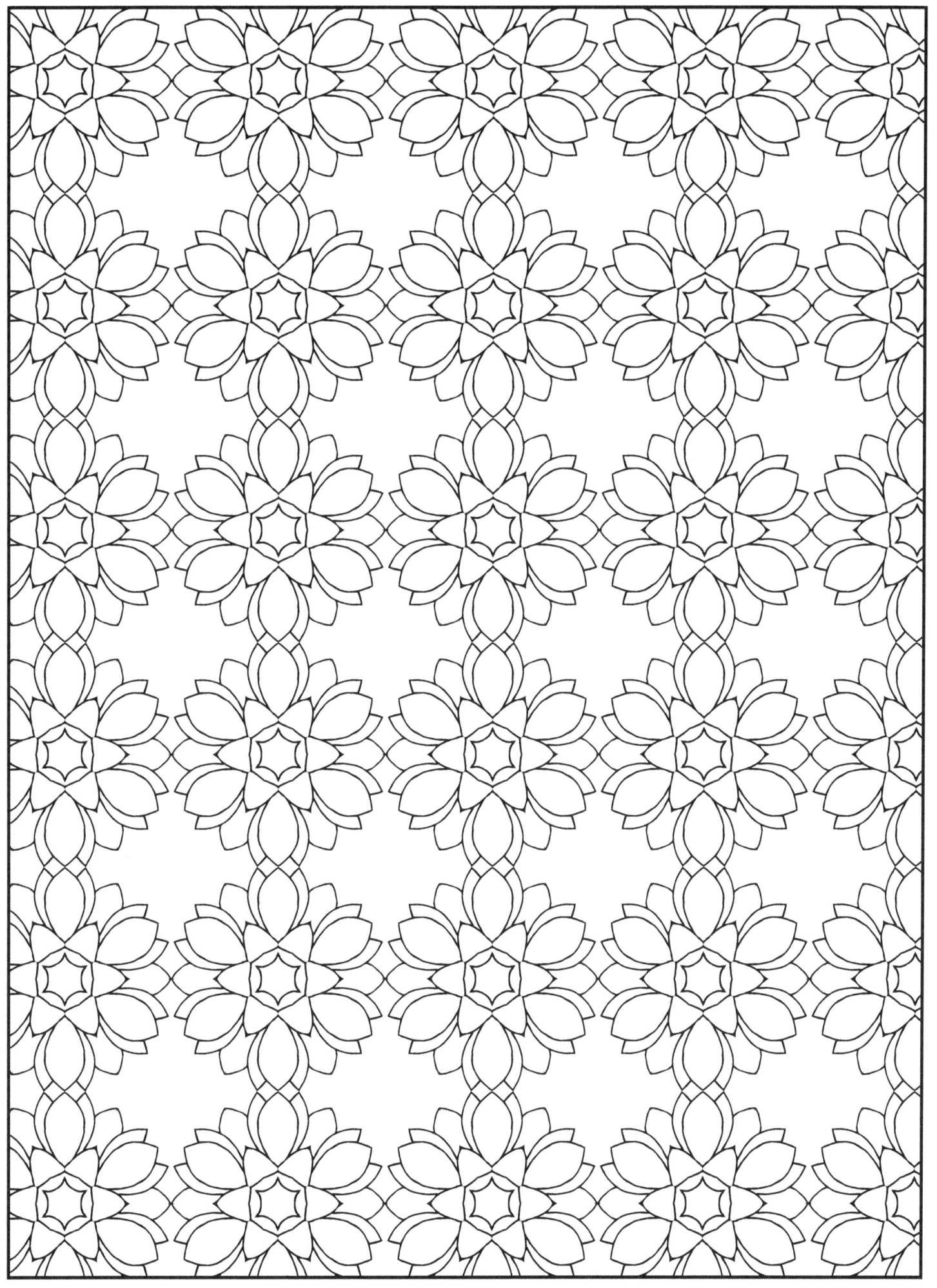

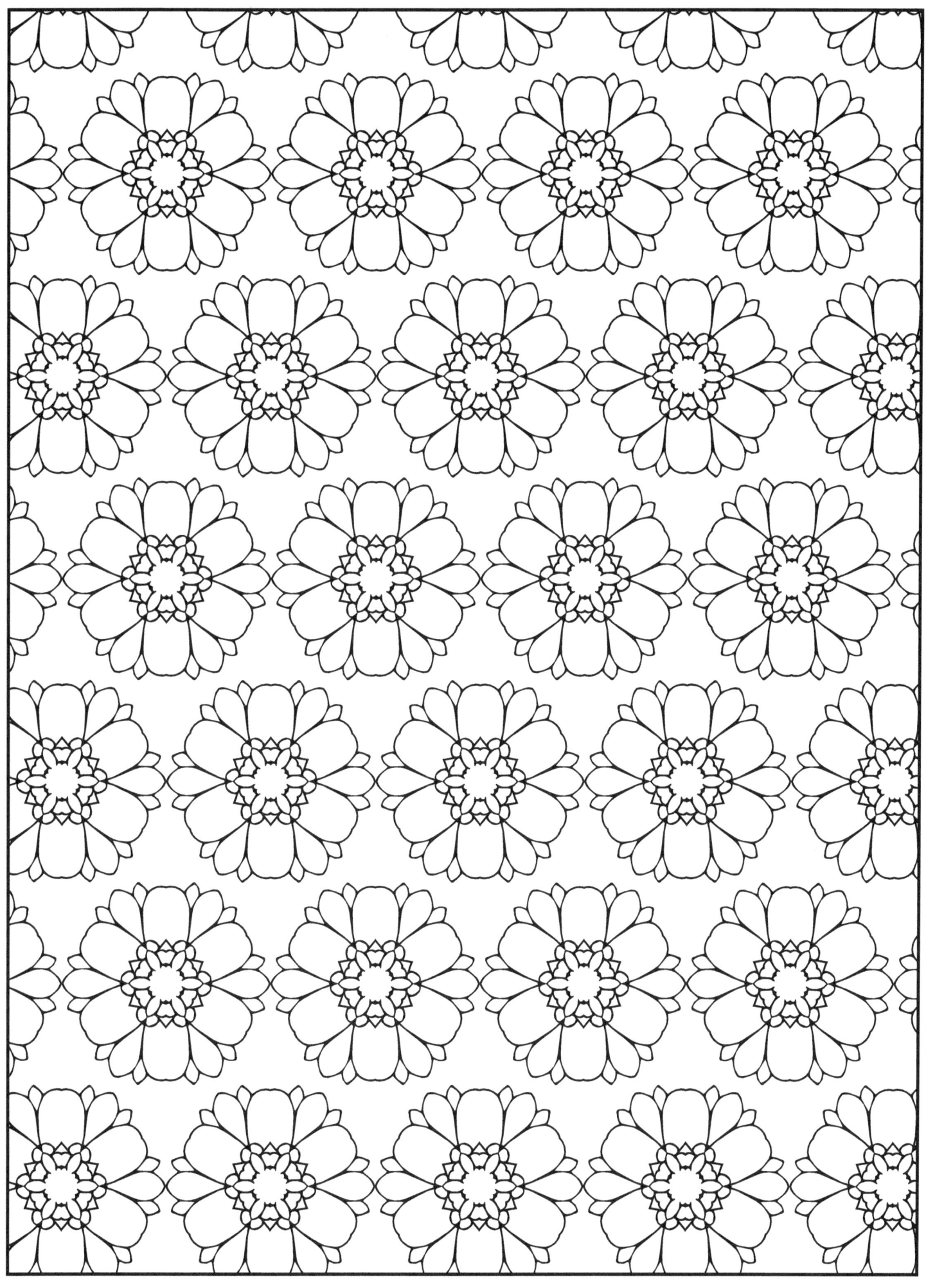

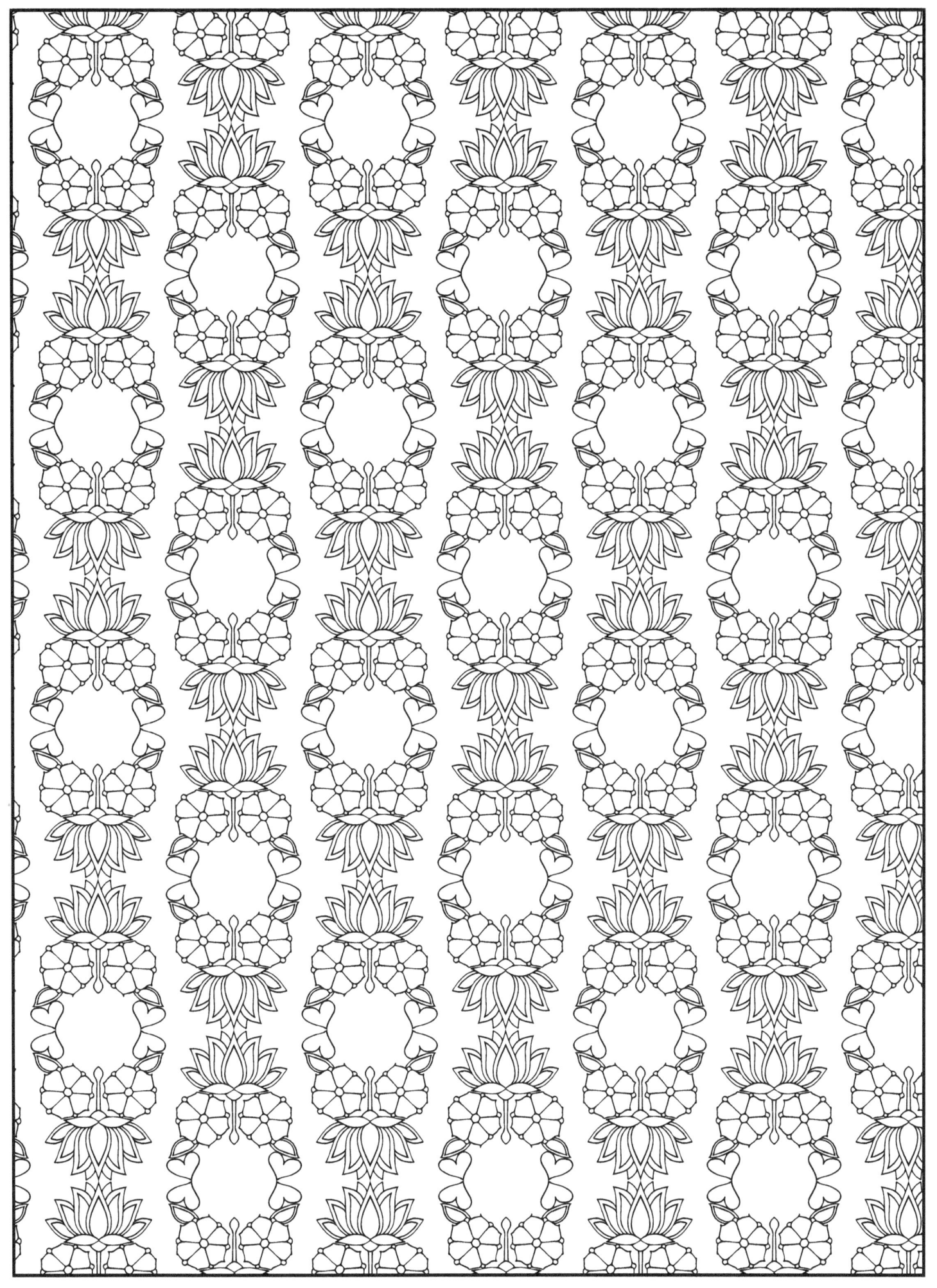

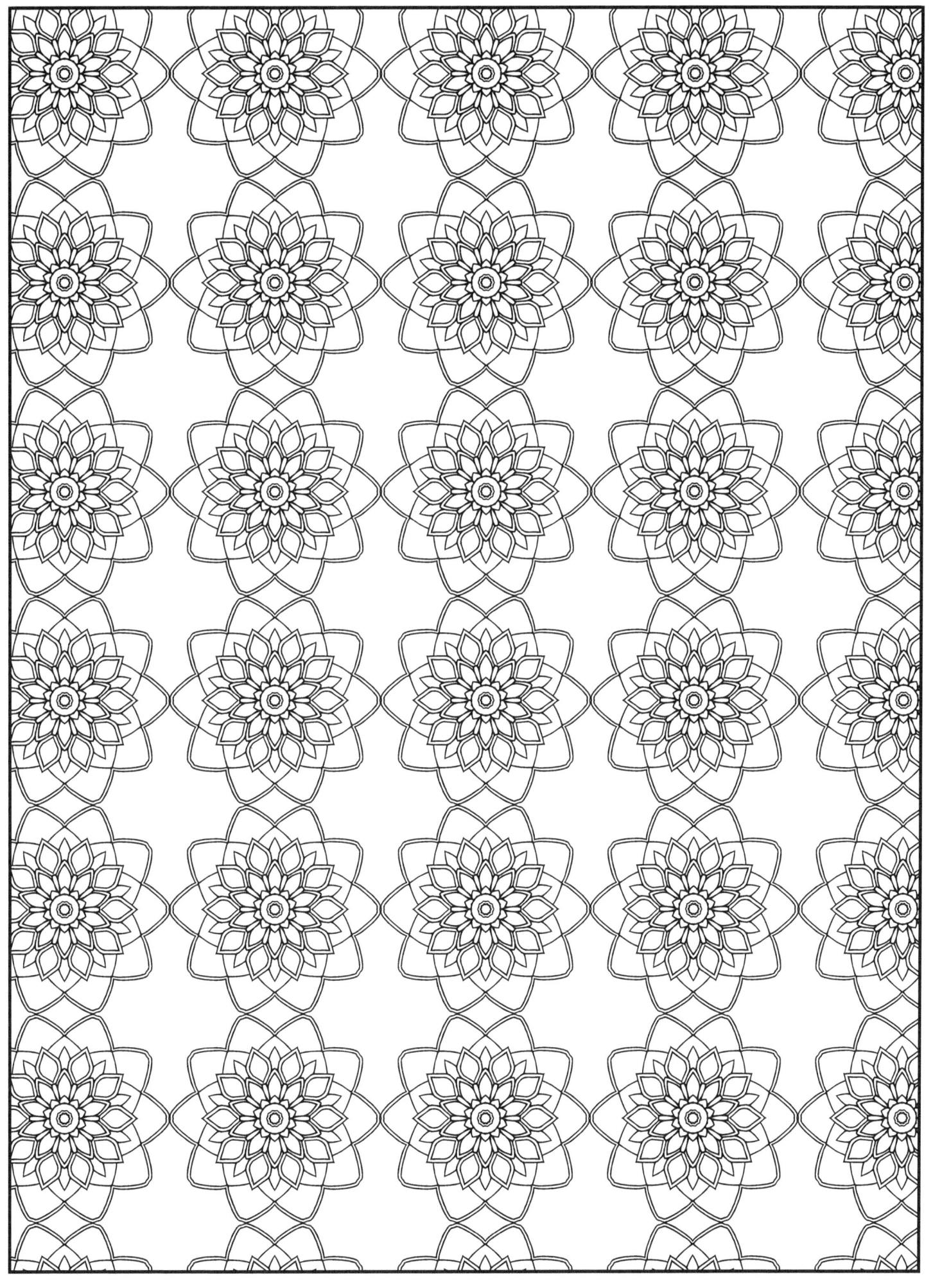

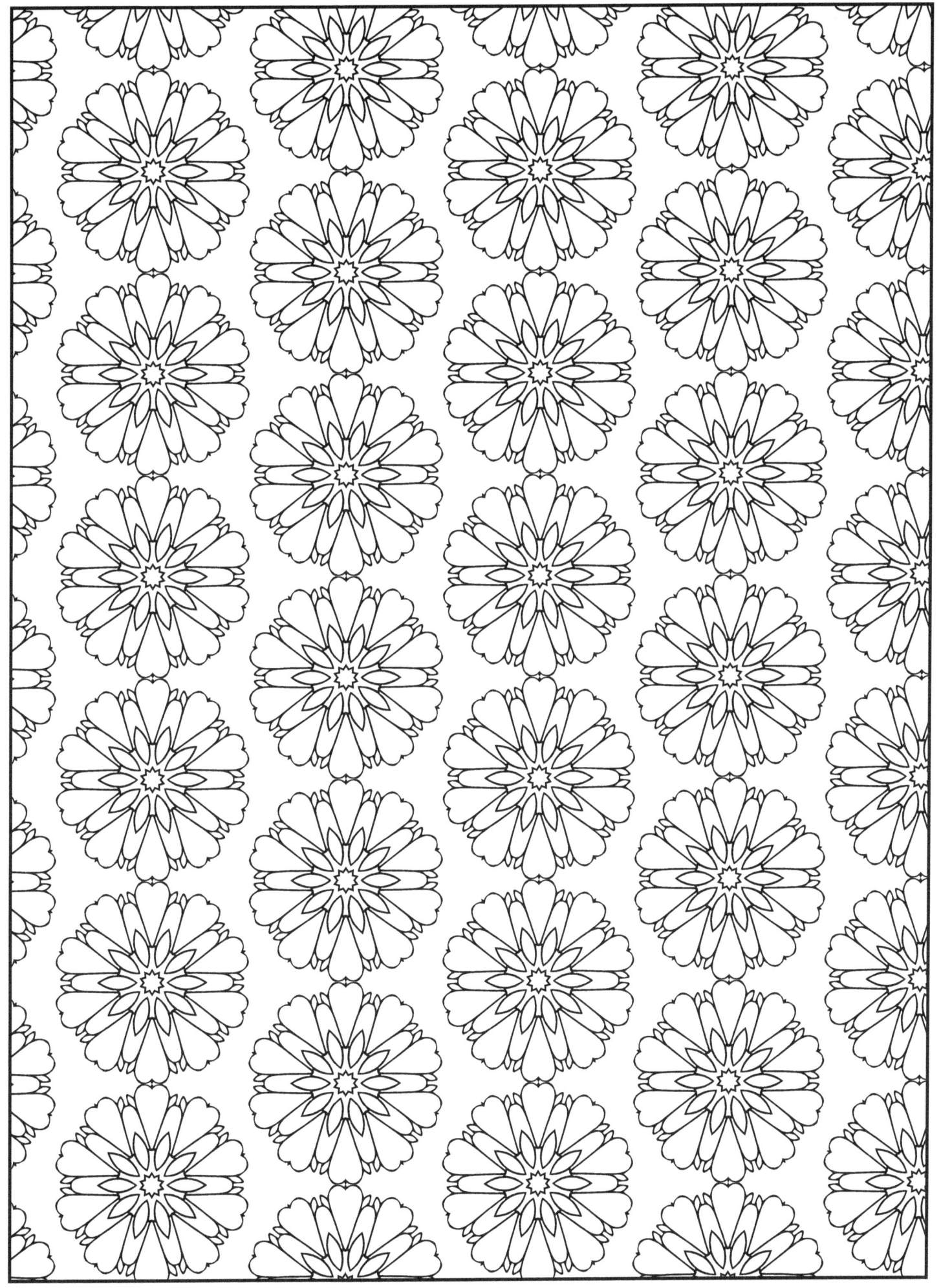

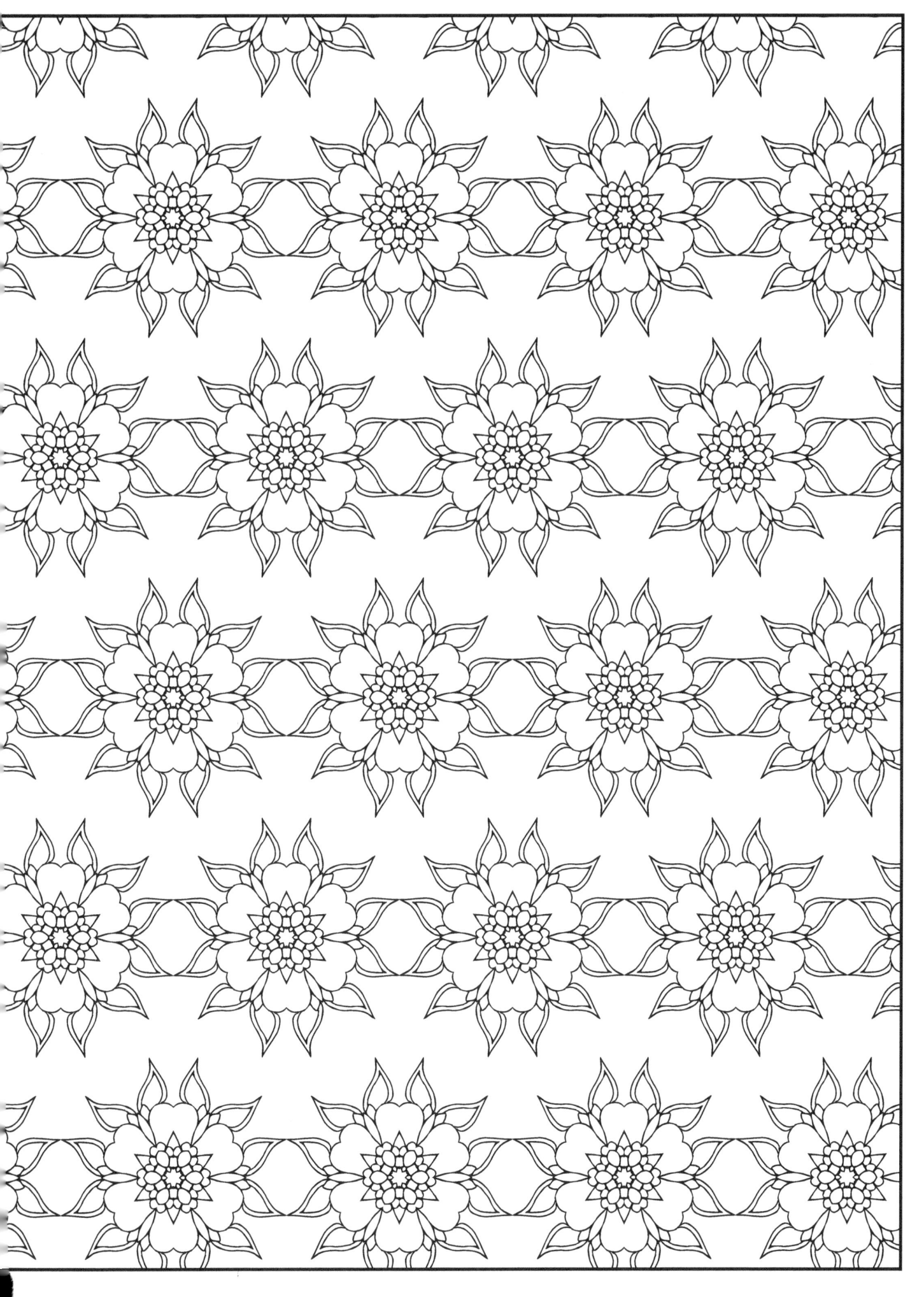